Momentary Madness

Momentary Madness

a collection of
poems
by

Mukesh Chhajer

Title: Momentary Madness
Author: Mukesh Chhajer
Language: English

Publisher: Mukesh Chhajer
Published: August 2012

Books by Mukesh Chhajer:
- Random Reflections (2006)
- On Life and Liberation: Essays on Jain Practices and Philosophy (2007)
- Silent Voices (2008, 2012)
- समय के रंग (Samay Ke Rang (in Hindi)) (2010, 2012)
- Tirthankar Mahaveer: A Biography in Verse (2010, 2012)
- Momentary Madness (2012)

Cover Design: Mukesh Chhajer

ISBN-13: 978-0615681801
ISBN-10: 0615681808

Part I

fantasies die, dreams
meet their demise when
the full moon becomes
the enemy of the night

bright-eyed or brooding
to assume even for a moment
that the moon is to enlighten
is to step into a quick-sand

moon is mischievous
its light is nefarious
illusion is its game
to fell, its purpose

dreams and fantasies can survive
only under the sun
moon merely lures them into
a greater darkness

ᛣ❋ᛤ

if I look beyond
the immediate horizon
the setting sun unveils
a strange darkness

pitched dark and blackest of the black
but the hue changes if
I have the patience to stay
still and let it reveal itself

thinning away the darkness
to display a rainbow
layer-by-layer
to bring forth a new dawn

the gift of the setting sun if
one just let it perform, its magic

days and nights, thoughts
invade the mind
to conquer the space
that was meant to be empty

the defenses are weak, crumbling walls
the intended support, never arrived
on one's own, challenge is terrifying
with others presence, defeat is ensured

to continue to fight, is a frightening thought
to give up now, is not an option
it is time to find, a new solution
before time plays its trick, once again

C�❀ಬ

in victory, there is arrogance
in defeat, there is shame
in love, one surrenders
without worrying about consequences

in business, it is profit
in career, promotion
at home, it is filial
outside, respect
in love, one surrenders
without weighing pros-and-cons

at work, it is professional
with friends, social
in public, it is dignity
in private, hesitation
in love, one surrenders
without any conditions

ॐ ❀ ॐ

never should one ask
what is your path
destinations have hijacked
life's essence

titles are bought, degrees sold
matters of importance, decided in the dark
higher the office, lower the standards
white clothes adore, dubious characters

closeness to power is, the measure of success
value of a man lies, in a stuffed envelope
lies are the fire-crackers, let them dance
truth is too subtle, to be observed at noon

ଓ❀ଅ

Mukesh Chhajer

within boundaries
joy is unbounded
without boundaries
fragmented and momentary

with eyes open
world is limited
with closed
the universe unfolds

with ears open
sound is important
with closed
silence reigns supreme

with mouth open
words dominate
with closed
one connects with the source

within boundaries
joy is unbounded

ଓଷ୍ଟ

nature has come to mourn
with thick dark clouds
joys that it once bestowed
shedding tears of sorrow

bountiful rain-drops
once invited heart-felt thanks
viewed a nuisance, now-a-days
man is too busy, plotting its own demise

generous fire
once the sustaining force
now being banished to
smolder in deep forests

plentiful air
once the life blood
today has become poisonous
to our own existence

nature is not jealous or angry
of man's progress, only
reminding man of
its misplaced priorities

೮ ❈ ೞ

the music of life is
not always sweet
irregular notes and harsh noises
sometimes, dominate

accept them with grace
or express displeasure
life is immune to
man's temper-tantrums

to arrive early or, to arrive late
nothing that matters will, ever be achieved
the time must be right and, place appropriate
life demands, an exact coincidence

ଓ ❀ ଃ

silence, the bane of excessive
exchange of words
goes unnoticed until mouth
becomes tired of its own chatter

silence, the underlying substratum
supports every form of communication
yet remains detached
and untouched

silence, the infinite sky
allows every motion, every gesture
only to render them
moot

silence, within and without
conflict of a single arrow
in mid-flight

silence is seeking an audience

ः॰ःः

walk, on those paths
that never were laid

smell the fragrance
that never could escape
the flower

bathe in the water
that never could flow out
of its source

breathe the air
that never was part
of another being

seek the goal
that never was stated
in clear terms

walk, on those paths
that never were laid

ॐ ✳ ॐ

terror has closed the hearts
politicians are eager to exploit
fear and irrationality that
people seek comfort in

it is a divide between, us and them
your position is a sign of, weakness or worse
those who see only in, black-and-white
forget that life is lived, only in grey

truth is subjected to, the test of loudness
politeness is considered, a debilitating weakness
in a world we claim to be, civilized and educated
stupidity and boorishness, pervades in every vein

opponent is now, a declared enemy
civility is being buried, repeatedly
family values have sprouted, a new strain
bigoted are those who, disagree with me

terrorists are trapped in, their own caves
and the rest of us have managed to, become unhinged
our hearts have become, the dwelling places
for the devil we, vehemently despise

ଔ❀ଔ

Mukesh Chhajer

nowhere is truth more evident
than in our own ugliness
denials have become the friends
who lead us to paths, unsavory

whether it is priests or parents
whether friends or siblings
the path that they lead us to
only slopes downward

boundaries of ethics and character
limits on moral behavior
leaving the burden on the world to define
we over-step as often as we can

heart forever closed and, the source of
compassion and love filled with dirty water
we only know how to distribute
the ugliness of a human soul

ദ ✿ ഏ

if darkness is not a part, of your life
then you are not human
if light has not yet entered, your heart
humanity has yet to incarnate

success and failure were
meant to be lessons
we have assigned them
different meanings

pleasure and pain were
meant to be companions
we have decided to
choose sides

the bridge to connect from
here to hereafter
has now become
a battle ground

without the support of
evenness
I hang by the strength
of my finger nails

ଔ❀ଓ

Mukesh Chhajer

racing toward the destination
with feet stuck in mud
we have learnt how to create
roadblocks for others, and for ourselves

organizations, rituals, procedures
bogged downed in rules and regulations
a white spotless dress has replaced
cleanliness of the heart

donate time, money and effort
to get a foothold in the society
counting bodies at the funeral
we forget, what is living

every smile is colored
every tear has a purpose
every word that leaves the lips
dripping with sweet poison

destination is a mirage
path itself is lost
stuck in mud, we only know
how to drag ourselves down

ಐ ❀ ೞ

we are at war
enemy is brutal and dangerous
must we do all
to be victorious

a battle cry that has filled
every pore of space
for last many-many years

once this enemy resided in
far-off caves, now it has
moved next door and, slowly
permeating into our every pore

but how can it resist the temptation
when we give it so much respect

☙❀❧

Mukesh Chhajer

dreams come and go
some get realized quickly, others vanish
to remain non-existent
then there are those who
refuse to fall in either category

constantly hounding without
sufficient energy, they
remain in a state of
suspended animation
a guerrilla warfare that achieves
little except hundreds of cuts

an impotent sun, in the middle of a winter
laughed at, by the tiny snow flakes
a drop of water, in a vast desert
in its futile attempt, to keep a thirsty man alive
a fire, trying to sustain itself
on a pool, of ice water

such are the dreams that
define life

03 ✿ 80

letter, phone, email, twitter
the pace of communication quickens every year
the promise of gratification that fuels the progress
remains unfulfilled as ever before

man's restlessness is increasing ever faster
victory and defeat are becoming the only measures
a moment's quiet is a wasted effort
collecting boxes is considered progress

the hunger to conquer the world is demonic
consuming humanity, at an alarming pace
never the man has stopped, to consider
the consequences of its own, cannibalistic tendencies

 CB❈80

Mukesh Chhajer

in the seriousness of my youth
I took a path few would consider wise
in the lightness of my adulthood
I am forced to admit, I was wrong

in the seriousness of my youth
I was too trusting
in the lightness of my adulthood
I have realized, it was a mistake

in the seriousness of my youth
I became idealistic
in the lightness of my adulthood
I have realized, it is impractical

in the seriousness of my youth
I wanted to change the world
in the lightness of my adulthood
I have realized, changing oneself should be the goal

in the seriousness of my youth
I wanted to see truth face-to-face
in the lightness of my adulthood
I have realized, absolute truth is an illusion

 CB ❀ 80

journeys take people
far and away
distances can be measured
in miles, and in tears

when a leaf is attached to a tree
restrictions make it angry
when separated, it can only
watch helplessly, its own decay

when a drop of water is a part of a river
restrictions make it angry
when separated, it can only
watch helplessly, its own decay

journeys take people
far and away
distances can be measured
in miles, and in tears

ᬘ❀ᬙ

truth is never revealed, in public
falsehood is never exposed, in isolation
man has not understood, the ways of the divine
a temple stands, at every street corner

worships are colorful and, buildings majestic
sermons are delivered with, emotions and passion
dancing and clapping, counts for devotion
the moisture though, never seeps within

the earth is dry, barren and sandy
no amount of water will, make it fertile
a raging inferno lies underneath
ready to destroy every, ounce of humidity

ᭃ❀ᭅ

without success, without happiness
life has encountered, crisis after crisis
one wonders what, memories to keep
every one comes, with a heavy price

to forget is blissful, a clean slate
future can be written, with little effort
without an anchor though, it remains uprooted
a dry leaf, caught in a hurricane

ride it does, on a raging wave
power though it has of, little to change
to befriend a bully is, never wise
a crushing burden, too heavy to bear

ଓ ❀ ଚ

plaid shirts and striped pants
models walking in a convoluted manner
to entice the unsuspecting consumers
to buy, happiness

a concept, invented by the civilized man
a fallacy, that never seems to get exposed
the society walks with eyes closed
who would dare admit, he has been fooled

ೞ❀ೞ

seeking glory, to embrace victory
war has become, the latest casualty

the traditional wisdom, war is evil
thrown overboard to establish, a new paradigm

pre-emptive strikes, divining the future
evil will be crushed, before its birth

a claim too often, in the annals of time
found itself trampled, under dying feet

C8❀80

with the past, that loves to haunt
and a future, that is fluid and uncertain
I am holding on to life, by a rope
as thick as a strand of hair

in a river, deep and turbulent
creating waves, with demonic powers
hungry to consume, every ounce of me
as I try to navigate, with my feeble hands

tossed around, on the water and on the ground
both are eager to, extract a revenge
for the time when, I used to sail
in a heavy boat, laden with goods

ೞ ❀ ೲ

from sunrise until sunset
mind is in a tailspin
unable to restrain itself, it
blurts out unsavory secrets

in person and in public
in gatherings of every type
it tells stories with
barely a kernel of truth

spiced up, tossed around
cooked on a fiery grill
the mind knows how to
spruce up a dull story

ন ✸ ন

Mukesh Chhajer

in a dance of life, no one is satisfied
every coin has, two sides

head or tail, it's a matter of chance
the other side is, not far behind

joys and sorrows, forever conjoined
victory and defeat, follow in sequence

mine and yours, a mere illusion
a breath can end, all claims to possessions

in a dance of life, no one is satisfied
every coin has, two sides

ꆩ❀ꆬ

Momentary Madness

when tears appear, can
a flood be far behind
devastation that ensues
words cannot describe

to the naked eyes
all will look alright
to fully understand
one must take, a step further

when the earth shook
and the heaven thundered
nothing in me moved
even an inch

the force of a tear though
is many times over
a tiny drop has the power
to move, the dense inner core

ଔ❀ଈ

Mukesh Chhajer

at dawn and at dusk
close eyes for a few moments
let the beauty of the nature, free and abundant
fill your every pore

dawn is a reminder that
darkness is temporary
how-so-ever deep, the sun
always returns

dusk is a reminder that
life is cyclic
high noon is but
a momentary phase

they come and they go
at regular intervals
you are present though
every moment of every day

enjoy your own eternity

ങ ✿ ഏ

caught in a cross-fire
casualty of a stray bullet
a collateral damage remains
an unaccounted number

claimed by neither side
street owns the dead body
lying abandoned, rotting
until it becomes a nuisance

then to be disposed off
unceremoniously
to be caught in a cross-fire
is the ultimate insult

03❀80

Mukesh Chhajer

inculcate, what you have not yet
embraced; distance, from that which
has become your second nature

become restless if silence
is the goal; remain content if
you wish to undertake a journey, long

every act, that you have become master of
will lead to your down fall, if performed
with an active participation

ॐ❀ॐ

heading home, the legs
are tense, mouth dry and
head swollen, an uncertain
welcome awaits

the news of victories
gains and conquests were
dispatched on the wings of air
the gory details, lag behind

conceit, debauchery and back-biting
that served so well in the field
now are ready to extract, their price

ᬧ❀ᬓ

together failed, alone conquered
the goal never left, any residue
to be utilized by the world
eager to make profit

when the call came, in the guise
of a failed attempt, the response
became counter-intuitive
exposing the cause of dissatisfaction

and removing the only obstacle
that had kept
the success bottled up

ଓ ✿ ଓ

drop the weapon, surrender
the battle you wage will
bring only suffering and pain

enemy is within, in conflict
an arrow cannot distinguish between
a foe and a friend

to unleash the fury
to uproot the tranquility
to upset the balance
requires only a momentary madness

ଓ ✾ ଅ

Mukesh Chhajer

in an attempt to control
what the nature has generously bestowed
man has come up trumps
with weapons of mass destruction

whether abuse of forests and rivers
whether abuse of air and space
whether abuse of man and animals
man has created innovative methods

don't underestimate though, man's generosity
it has vowed to preserve, nature's diversity
all those who man forced, to the edge of extinction
it would provide them an abode, in liquid nitrogen

 CX❋XO

hot tea, a substantive addition
of heat and energy to an
otherwise dull metabolic system
in early morning

as the warm liquid runs down
the throat and the subsequent passages
waking them up to get ready
for more strenuous and difficult tasks
that lie ahead, but for the moment
just makes them feel elated

and the stomach, that has not seen
food for some time, eagerly welcomes
another guest to share its bounty
of acids and alkaline

and the exit system, shut down
since the previous night, once again
finds itself active and ready to perform
essential functions, for the continuation of life

just a hot cup of tea !!!

03 ❀ 80

Mukesh Chhajer

past, present or future
no one knows what comes first
mind cannot comprehend
tied with countless memories

time is an illusionist
likes to play a few tricks
a few strokes on a canvas
give an impression of a flowing river

can it though satisfy thirst, can it
take one to a far away destination
a river on a canvas is
as dead, as the painter

ೞ ❀ ೞ

fire that emanates from
the center of the earth
burns only the dross that
covers the surface

slow and steady, unspectacular
to bring out the colors
one at a time without
leaving behind a carnage

all other fires are
mere show-offs

೮೮ ❀ ೮೮

Mukesh Chhajer

unable to explain the past
or divine the future
man has learnt how
to defeat the truth

every question that arises
can be unexplained by
a nod, a twitch or a silence

every answer that
can be obfuscated
will find a full expression

every truth seeking light
will be buried under
a mountain of debris

caught in the trap of time
man has found an escape
cheating life of its
most meaningful ingredients

છ ✿ ૭

the vanishing darkness with
the approaching dawn
every ray beats back a ton
of depression, to raise
hope and happiness after
a long-long slumber

don't though go overboard
use the time, generously afforded
by the fragile hours of the early morning
to understand the full spectrum
of human conditions before
the blinding brightness once again
turns life one dimensional

೧෴೧

Mukesh Chhajer

darker than the black hole
we carry within ourselves
to witness darkness
in bright day light

brighter than the sun
we carry within ourselves
to witness light
in the middle of a moonless night

to merely focus on that
which is easy to point to
we spend life worrying about
things, unimportant

ಚ ❁ ಖ

thoughts, never the ones
to stay behind, have suddenly
disappeared without
any reason

mind, without its usual
companion, feels lost
broken and without
foundation

an existential crisis
for which the mind was
never, prepared

03 ❀ 80

Mukesh Chhajer

whether alone or in company
my task is clear
the struggle I face cannot
be shared by others

the fears are mine and so are the challenges
the happiness I seek must, spring from within
for too long have I, let others be the judge
the cycle that has led, only to crises

now is the time, and today is the day
to break the cycle, and move away
for every path that, goes unrepeated
a new one appears, to support the life

છ❀ો

when a tear appears, one
feels uncertain
what brings it, what does it mean

joy-sorrow, happiness-sadness
or just an irritant in the eyes
sweet memories or hard past
or a clever instrument of deceit

poor tear, becoming an unwitting
pawn in the game played by man
to amuse itself and the world

ೞ ❀ ೞ

Mukesh Chhajer

pieces of life, scattered
across the oceans and beyond
no words can convince them
to join together, once again

an existence that spans
the universe, I had heard
is the ultimate achievement
no one though warned, it could
be excruciatingly painful
if the pieces do not fall
at the right locations

 CG ✻ ୫୦

a question arose then got
pushed away, the answer
followed after a considerable delay

questions and answers, too many
to keep track of, straws in
a flood do not build a house
by themselves

stones, mighty and strong, remain
worthless without a mason
unrestrained fires in a forest
only bring greater destruction

questions and answers are
substances of the living if they
can be arranged in a
coherent pattern

ಚ ✻ ಜ

it is November and Thanksgiving
is upon us, the official start
of Christmas shopping season

long-lines, early in the morning
daring rain and cold, the thought
of a cheap computer, camera
television or home appliance trumps
a few moments of
quiet contemplation

God waits in line
for His turn to be acknowledged
while man fills up the cart
on this Black Friday

ೞ ❀ ೦

stand up but be aware
the ground beneath is not strong enough
to support the weight of lies
that life has become

surrender and remember
a river always finds a way
to reach its destination even
if it has to overcome a thousand hurdles

൬ ❀ ൭

O spirit, fly away to those
regions of the universe that are
uninhabited and silent

promises of this life while
enticing and ego boosting
are mere pittance if you
could separate yourself just
for a moment, from yourself

the clarity of thoughts and mind
in a place that has never been polluted
by the human greed and passions
can turn even an animal in to
a divine being

O spirit, fly away
without delay

ଓଛ❀ଓ

a ray of light that filtered
through a glass window and
curtains, having traveled
through a space of infinite
expanse, breathed its last
on a wooden plank, momentarily
lighting the surrounding room

followed by the next and
the next and the next until
one could not see the individual sacrifices
filling the room with, bright light

second-by-second, minute-by-minute
day-by-day, year-by-year
I have watched the ultimate
sacrifice without remorse
until the moment of

my last breath to realize
the courage it takes to
die so that others can continue
their lives, without interruptions

చ ❀ ಊ

in streets of Kabul, in mountains of Tora-Bora
in slums and palaces of, Baghdad and Basra
in Mumbai, Madrid, London and New York
an abode exists, for a continuous war

enemies are arrayed, in close quarters
eyeing each other, through a cross-hair
a finger on the trigger, and hatred in heart
ready to pounce, without a thought

a bullet passes through, a filled stomach
another passes through, an empty heart
a thundering cloud, engulfs the sky
detaching a many, bodies from the soul

enemies now stand, face-to-face
eager to annihilate, each other
hands though theirs are, devoid of power
without the weapons, once so dear

untethered fog, in the sky
quickly losing sense, of their being
swearing in hearts, without beating
they vow to avenge, unto eternity

03 ❀ 80

is it Christmas-season or
that of holidays
offending each other has
become the new pastime
the two sides though are
in unison on this
thank Almighty, for
the best possible deals

early morning openings and late night sales
legs are unable to support, the extra carried weight
thanks to the Almighty though, we shall endure
Lord has bestowed us with, insatiable appetite

through busy malls and, crowded streets
through long lines and, countless traffic jams
with bags of goodies and, beaming faces
we thank Lord for his, generous offerings

ᨏ ❋ ᨐ

when the mouth is closed
and eyes shut
when every pore of the body
forgets itself
you have arrived

the journey may have been
long or short
the hurdles may have appeared
insurmountable or non-existent
when the knowledge is revealed and
"the difference between" becomes
a meaningless phrase
you have arrived

when sweetness and bitterness, comingle
when hatred and love, lose themselves
when richness and poorness, become one
when thoughts and mind, disappear
you have arrived

wake up, the moment is near

ॐ ❀ ॐ

don't wake me up
I have learnt to
live in the darkness

creating a world that
I wish to experience
I enjoy and suffer
at the vagaries of my mind

creating a world with
grains of sand, I
mold it constantly
in to my own image

tears of joy and, that of sorrow
bails of laughter but, no one to share
the company I keep is, full of puppets
I scurry around in, fake importance

ಚ಼ 🌼 ಜ

Mukesh Chhajer

truth stares but our eyes
cannot bear, keeping shut
mind is eager to find an explanation
it will find, convenient

convoluted arguments, ignored facts
half-truths mixed with, unsubstantiated
claims, and lo we have arrived
at the desired conclusions

shed light if you wish to
be thrown in to the hell, for eternity

ॐ ❀ ॐ

keep truth at a distance
until you have developed
a coat strong enough to withstand
the ensuing heat it brings

the cool comfort of the falsehood
though despised is essential
for those who wish to exist
as mere mortals

೦ﾟ❀ ೲ

Mukesh Chhajer

under the coat of darkness
when no one was watching
nature donned itself
with clothes, most divine

every tree branch, every blade of grass
every speck of dust, every inch of naked earth
graced with a smile, most divine

every bird, every squirrel, every raccoon
every deer, every lion, and the moon
every river, every mountain, every man
embraced the silence, most divine

ॐ ❀ ॐ

Part II

death is a master if you
let it control life
a slave, otherwise

friendship is just a myth
death uses to ensnare
those gullible enough

ᥳ❀ᥲ

Mukesh Chhajer

curly or straight
hairs are easy to manage
the head they sit on
that's another matter

ॐ❀ॐ

if you extend a hand, be prepared
to be rejected if not bitten
acceptance depends on the others
state of mind

෩ ✾ ෨

Mukesh Chhajer

O truth, why are you so intransigent
a little compromise will go a long way
to make life easy and comfortable

ଔ ✿ ଓ

don't use the Book to
beat up on others
this Book was given, for
you to look within

ભ૰ઙૄ

Mukesh Chhajer

sooner or later, we will
come to the same fold
the time in between is the opportunity
to straighten a few wrinkles

ঙ ❀ ৫

planets and stars, forever on a run
to reach a destination, unknown

man though can, do one better
if it can remain, humble

ೞ❀ೡ

Mukesh Chhajer

I am trying real hard
to lose a battle
to set stage for
coming together

the other side though insists on
continuing the mayhem
end of the hostility will force it
to come face-to-face, with itself

ॐ ✻ ॐ

don't wake up if
the truth is being told
a little lie goes a long way
to put a smile on the face

ᛣ ✴ ᛤ

truth has never been measured
falsehood also remains unweighed
yet at every street corner
their followers stand ready
to slit each others throats

೧ ❀ ೮

instant success and instant failure
a world where a second is too long
a constant need to seek approval
the inner compass has broken into pieces

ભ☀ॐ

Mukesh Chhajer

God never meant to interfere
but man is forcing Him to choose
unweaving the fabric of life
one thread at a time

ॐ ❀ ॐ

untilled soil
littered with seeds
how can nature though
work its magic

ଔ ✻ ଓ

Mukesh Chhajer

expectations and burdens
we carry them at our own peril
bricks of different colors

❁

in a one-shot life where
success is not guaranteed
temptations are aplenty
to take short-cuts

temples, churches, mosques
and synagogues thrive
as man slides to collect
fake bounty

ೞ✺ೞ

don't look back, the regrets will
overwhelm
don't look ahead, the expectations will
consume
eyes firmly focused, on the moment
remain absorbed
past and future are merely illusions
to catch one off-guard

ॐ ❀ ॐ

death is neither a friend
nor a foe
death is just a stop on a journey
that began a long-long ago

೫❀೩

Mukesh Chhajer

no breath goes waste but
the one who breathes
does not recognize its value
until it is too late

☙ ❀ ❧

a drop of sweat and that of tear
mix together to journey down the cheek
with an uncertain past and an uncertain future
the tremors quickly, reach the heart

will it remain intact or pay
the ultimate price

ॐ✻ॐ

Mukesh Chhajer

a broken window, a work of art
a crumbling wall, a sight to behold
a dilapidated building, a picture of beauty
every misfortune is an opportunity, in someone's eyes

ౠ✿౭

sign of distress when one
cannot be by oneself
two is a duality, not
a state of perfection

03 ❀ 80

Mukesh Chhajer

the refrain is, one must find a balance
no one asks, why did you tie yourself
with two extreme ends

ॐ✺ॐ

with two weak hands, one can
lift a heavy weight
with two weak legs, one can
walk a thousand miles
with two weak ears, one can
hear songs of praise
with two weak eyes, one can
witness beauty of the world
if one can keep one mouth
shut and one mind under control

 og ❀ ಬ

Mukesh Chhajer

with mask on the face and
a sword in hand
the urge to decapitate
propels one to center stage

the enemy stands, bound and gagged
weak in knees and fearful in eyes
but the sword refuses to strike
because the face in front resembles the one
that the mask hides

ෆ❀ౚ

behind or ahead, how
is one to judge when
all the milestones have
disappeared

೦ಇ ✿ ಹಿಂ

Mukesh Chhajer

in my own little cavern, I
have found the resources
that can keep me alive
for a long-long time

an existence that even death
would not be jealous of

ଔ ❀ ଓ

walk in the shadows, the bright
light brings flaws into
sharp focus

೮ ✻ ೮

Mukesh Chhajer

the sun, overshadowed by a cloud
a tree or a leaf
the mighty sun, defeated
by its own progenies

that's how nature works
but man has learnt to upstage
its own future

ಚ ❀ ಬ

don't
walk away from the darkness
that is not you

just open the eyes

ଔ✸ଌ

truth never struggles
falsehood is always pretending
but man knows how
to sweeten that
which is unpalatable
creating cancer

ॐ ❀ ॐ

is the pace too fast
or too slow
is the effort too little
or over the top

have you learnt how to stir the pot
merely holding the ladle
is not going to produce
the soup, most delicious

೫ ❀ ೞ

Mukesh Chhajer

ghosts, not the ones who
lurk in the dark, have
taken over, turning
life in to darkness

ೞ❀ಬ

unsheathe
the sword but be
prepared to face its judgment

a sword once out of sheath
will not return without
tasting blood

ॐ❀ॐ

Mukesh Chhajer

if you can close a door, don't
if you can open a door, don't
an illusion is always an illusion
how-so-ever it makes its entrance

ॐ ✿ ॐ

celebrate but remember
commiserate but remember
mourn but remember
what use holding on to that
which is transient

಩ ❀ ಞ

Mukesh Chhajer

when the two come together
an outcome is engendered
will a one will emerge or splintered
pieces will be the result

 CB ❀ ꙮ

without hope, life
is a pleasure
with hope, comes
despair

03 ✽ 80

Mukesh Chhajer

a rope with two ends, always
has a middle
tie the two together if you
wish to transcend

છ❀ಬ

there is no need to wait
push the door open
the world is never ready
to embrace, a bitter truth

ଓ ❀ ଚ

Mukesh Chhajer

wake up before dawn
the darkness can be
enlightening

the harsh light of the sun
drives away the subtle
signs of inner change

ఇ❀ఔ

Buddha is much admired today
and so is Gandhi
the world knows how to insult
a decent man

౦౩❀౭౦

Mukesh Chhajer

denounce, proclaim, announce
not much will it amount to if
the words that emerge from the mouth
did not emanate from deep down

ಲ ✺ ಬ

deep under the sea, inside
a hard shell, a tiny drop
of water has transformed itself
in to a beautiful pearl after
a thousand years of meditation

ଓ❀ଛ

Mukesh Chhajer

darkness or light, none
can show you the path
if the eyes within, are
closed

೧❁೩

truth dies, every moment
at home, at work, in
wide open world

falsehood lives in a fortress
guarded by an army, impenetrable

safety first, leaves no other choice

08 ❀ 80

heard enough, read enough
now you must confess
the knowledge that you gleamed through
amounts to pittance

ॐ ✺ ॐ

when the morning came
it only promised to remove
the cover of darkness
don't blame it for
what is revealed

ଔ❀ଓ

Mukesh Chhajer

remember the summer when
you declared, "I am in love"
remember the winter
that followed, chilling every bone
remember the smile that
melted your every pore
and the silent glare that
froze every drop of blood
the dark and light fringes
hide more than they reveal

 C3❀80

truth will be revealed
when the walls of falsehood
will crumble under its own weight
within oneself

Mukesh Chhajer

call not, but listen
a loud noise will drown away
the wisdom from within

 C3 ❀ 80

every change suffers from
the possibility that it will
become, permanent

 Cʒ ❀ ꙅꙩ

Mukesh Chhajer

a cleansing ritual to rid
the world of infidels
creating an exodus through
a river of blood

క్ష ✿ శం

beyond and before, comes
the true challenge
recognize and realize
to attain the perfection

ෆ❀ඏ

Mukesh Chhajer

when death comes, do
not be upset
when life comes, do
not celebrate
how can one hold on
to a dawn or a dusk
beyond a momentary
instant

ಣ ❀ ಜ

when it will be decreed
that you henceforth shall
become non-existent
do not protest
the honor thus bestowed

ॐ ❀ ॐ

www.ingramcontent.com/pod-product-compliance
Lightning Source LLC
Chambersburg PA
CBHW061746020426
42331CB00006B/1376